MATT CHRISTOPHER

In the Huddle with ...

John Elway

MATT CHRISTOPHER

In the Huddle with ...
John Elway

Little, Brown and Company
Boston   New York   London

First Edition

Library of Congress Cataloging-in-Publication Data

Christopher, Matt.
      In the huddle with . . . John Elway / Matt Christopher. — 1st ed.
            p.   cm.
      Summary: Examines the personal life and football career of the quarterback for the Denver Broncos.
      ISBN 0-316-13355-8
      1. Elway, John, 1960–   — Juvenile literature.   2. Football players — United States — Biography — Juvenile literature.
3. Denver Broncos (Football team) — Juvenile literature.   [1. Elway, John, 1960–   .   2. Football players.]   I. Title.
GV939.E48C57   1999
796.332'092 — dc21
[B]   98-45549

10 9 8 7 6 5 4 3 2 1

COM-MO

Printed in the United States of America

Contents

MATT CHRISTOPHER

In the Huddle with...

WITHDRAWN

Chapter One:
1960-1975

Birth of a Quarterback

John Elway was born to play quarterback.

His grandfather, Henry Elway, played quarterback for the University of Pennsylvania in 1908. In those days, players wore little padding and were rarely replaced during a game. You had to be tough to play, and Henry Elway was tough.

John's father, Jack Elway, also played football. He was a star in high school, and as a freshman quarterback at the University of Washington, he seemed to be on his way to a stellar collegiate career before a leg injury forced him to the sidelines.

But despite those bloodlines, John Elway, the Super Bowl–winning quarterback of the Denver Broncos and one of the greatest quarterbacks in professional football history, didn't have it easy. He worked long and hard to fulfill his unlimited potential, overcoming a series of setbacks to turn a career that was once marked by disappointment and frustration into one that has earned him the nickname the Comeback Kid. Because as anyone who follows football knows, John Elway is at his best precisely at the time when everything looks the worst. Just ask the Green Bay Packers about Super Bowl XXXII.

Many of the characteristics that have made John Elway one of the greatest players in football came from his father. After Jack Elway was forced to abandon his playing career, it would have been easy for him to become bitter and forget about the game altogether. But he didn't. When he learned that his playing career was over, he didn't give up on a life in football. He decided to become a coach and put the energy he once put into playing football into learning as much about the game as he could.

After graduating from college, Jack began pursuing his dream. He was named head coach at Port Angeles High School in Washington in 1953.

Soon after that he met a young woman named Janet and in 1957 they married and decided to start a family. Jack looked forward to having another El-way continue the family's football tradition.

First, the young couple had a daughter, Lee-Ann. The Elways were thrilled. Eighteen months later, on June 28, 1960, Janet Elway had twins, a girl and a boy. The Elways named the girl Janna and the boy John.

Although Janet Elway often teased Jack that all he ever thought about was football, she knew that his family was important to him, too. Whenever possible, she and the children attended games and practices, roaming the sidelines and spending time together.

Each fall, Jack put in long hours running practices and studying the game. He didn't want to be a high school coach forever. His goal was to become a head coach at a major college or in the National Football League.

In 1961, Jack got his first collegiate coaching job, at tiny Grays Harbor Community College. The family moved from Port Angeles, Washington, to Aberdeen, Washington, as Jack pursued his career.

That move was the first of many the Elways would

eventually make because of football. Young coaches, particularly those as ambitious and committed as Jack Elway, are always looking to move up in the coaching ranks. The Elways became accustomed to moving.

Like most young boys, John Elway looked up to his father. And no matter how busy Jack Elway was, he always tried to find time to spend with his son.

Not surprisingly, much of their time together was spent playing sports. Even before John had started school, he could throw and hit a baseball, dribble a basketball, and throw a football. Jack later told a reporter, "When John was little, he was always intrigued by balls."

In the backyard of the family home, John and his father would pretend to be famous professional athletes. When Jack would throw batting practice to John, he would announce the game like it was on the radio. "Dad was always the pitcher, announcer, and umpire," John says.

John would pretend it was the last game of the World Series and that he was a star like Mickey Mantle or Willie Mays trying to hit the game-winning home run. When they played football together, it was the same thing: As Jack chased his son around the yard, John would pretend he was a famous running back.

Although sports were important to Jack Elway, he tried not to push his son into athletics, for he knew that that strategy often backfired. But he need not have worried. John loved playing sports as much as he loved spending time with his father.

After John began attending school, he could hardly wait for the school day to end. Often his father would pick him up and take him to his offices at the gym at Grays Harbor, where John would get to run around and play with some of the players.

After six years at Grays Harbor, Jack Elway accepted a position at the University of Montana. Even though he was just an assistant, the job was a step up for Jack. The school faced much better competition. The family moved from Washington to Missoula, Montana.

When John was in the fourth grade, he began playing competitive football. Jack Elway knew his son was a good athlete, and faster than most boys his age. But he had no idea if John had a future as a football player.

John's team was called the Little Grizzlies. At practice before the season, the team's coach noticed how fast John ran and made him a running back.

When the Little Grizzlies played their first game, Jack Elway had to miss the beginning of the game due to a conflict with his coaching duties at the university. But as soon as he was free, he raced to the field.

He saw the two teams gathered in the end zones, resting. It was halftime.

Jack spotted his friend Jud Heathcote on the sidelines. Heathcote, who later became head basketball coach at Michigan State and coached Magic Johnson, was Montana's basketball coach. His son played for the Little Grizzlies, too.

Jack Elway ran up to Heathcote and breathlessly asked, "What did I miss?"

Heathcote smiled and shook his head, "Well, Jack," he said, "either every kid on that field is the worst player I've ever seen, or your boy is the greatest player I've ever seen." In the first half of his first game, John Elway had scored four touchdowns!

At the time, John's favorite football player was Calvin Hill, the star running back for the Dallas

Cowboys. John wore Hill's number and even began calling himself Calvin Elway.

Against the other peewee league players, John might as well have been Calvin Hill. No one could catch him. He was the best player in the league.

John and his father soon began taking sports more seriously. In the summer and during school vacations, John started attending sports camps for baseball, football, and basketball. He was good at all the sports. One basketball camp was operated by George Raveling, who late became known as one of the best coaches in collegiate basketball. When John was only twelve, he was such a good basketball player that Raveling tried to persuade Jack Elway to have his son focus only on basketball.

But Jack Elway didn't want to do anything that might dampen his son's enthusiasm toward sports. He knew John enjoyed playing everything and that it was much too early for John to concentrate on a single sport.

By the time John entered junior high school, the family had moved back to Washington, where Jack had accepted an assistant coaching position at Washington State University in Pullman. He was developing a reputation as an excellent coach and re-cruiter whose particular expertise was the passing game. Jack Elway loved to have strong-armed quarterbacks who could really throw the football.

As John reached adolescence, he experienced a growth spurt. His body began changing from a young boy's into a young man's. That is often an awkward time for a young athlete. Many children lose their coordination as they try to keep pace with their rapidly changing bodies.

Since John was playing so many sports, and playing so often, he was able to retain his coordination. But he got taller and heavier. Suddenly, the young boy who called himself Calvin Hill and ran circles around his peers wasn't the fastest boy on the field anymore. Although he still ran well, other boys were faster.

With a nudge from his father, John abandoned his dreams of becoming the next Calvin Hill and adopted a new hero, Cowboy quarterback Roger Staubach. On the baseball field, John had the strongest arm around, and John's father thought that quarterback was the only position on the football field that could take full advantage of his son's talent.

John easily handled the adjustment to quarterback. Just by being around his father, he had a grasp of the game that few other junior high players had. That, combined with his strong arm and overall athleticism, made quarterback the perfect position for him to play.

He was an instant star. Few junior high quarterbacks anywhere could throw a football as far or as accurately as John Elway. The only problem was finding someone to catch his passes. John threw so hard that the other boys sometimes had a hard time catching the ball!

Even Jack was impressed. He saw now that his son had the potential to be a very, very good quarterback. As a joke, Jack Elway filled out a scouting report on his son for the Dallas Cowboys, for whom he occasionally worked as a part-time scout.

The report read, "He's 6-2, 185 pounds, has a good arm, good speed, good agility. But he has a bad attitude because he didn't clean the swimming pool."

Except for the crack about John's attitude, in just a few years Jack Elway's assessment of his son would be eerily accurate.

A quarterback was born.

Chapter Two:
1975-1978

The First Comebacks

By the time John reached high school, the family was on the move again. In 1975, Jack was offered a head coaching job at the University of California at Northridge, usually referred to as Cal State–Northridge.

He couldn't turn down the opportunity. Although Cal State–Northridge didn't have much of a reputation in football, Jack Elway would finally get to be a head coach. And if he succeeded, he knew there was a good chance he would be noticed by a larger school.

But he didn't ignore his family. He wanted to move to a place where his children would be happy and challenged.

He researched high schools in the Northridge area for one that had a superior academic record as well as a football program that focused on the passing game. He even interviewed the coaches. Jack finally decided on Granada Hills High School, a school with a stellar athletic and academic reputation. Coach Jack Neumeier used an innovative, pro-style offense; his team sometimes passed the ball 50 or 60 times a game. Jack quickly found a house in the area and the family moved to Granada Hills.

The children began attending Granada Hills in the fall of 1975. During his freshman year, John played for the junior varsity football team. Despite his skill at throwing the football, John was still growing. He was only about five foot ten and 150 pounds, too small and slender to make the varsity team.

Even so, it was obvious to everyone that Granada Hills had an emerging prodigy at quarterback. Nearly every game, John threw several touchdown passes. And despite his small stature, some of his throws sailed more than 60 yards through the air! Many college quarterbacks can't throw that far.

With the help of his father and his coaches at Granada Hills, John became serious about football. He studied films of games so he could learn to read defenses, and he made hundreds of practice throws every day. He even worked on the little things, like his footwork and the way he dropped back after taking the ball from the center.

But the Elways never let him forget that he was a student, too. John had to do his homework, and he knew that any grade below a "B" was unacceptable. Math was his favorite subject. He wrote for the school newspaper, covering — what else? — sports.

John continued to play other sports in addition to football. Although he eventually abandoned basketball, he played baseball for his school team, becoming a powerful hitter, star third baseman, and occasional pitcher.

In 1976, at the beginning of his sophomore year, John looked forward to making the varsity football team. He did, but an older, more experienced player beat him out for the starting position at quarterback. John was frustrated, but he didn't get angry. He just kept working hard at practice and tried to improve a little bit every day.

The team got off to a poor start. They lost their first three games.

Coach Neumeier decided it was time for a change.

With thoughts of building for the future, he inserted some younger players into the starting lineup. One of those players was quarterback John Elway.

Although the team still struggled as the younger players gained experience, John was sensational. The promise of his powerful arm more than made up for his occasional mistakes. Neumeier was particularly impressed that when John did make an error, he worked doubly hard to make sure he didn't make the same mistake again. He was just as intense in practice as he was during a game.

The Granada Hills Highlanders were a young but experienced team when they took the field in the fall of 1977, John's junior year. With John leading the way, they were soon one of the most formidable teams in southern California.

John passed close to 300 yards in almost every game. Although the Highlanders' defense was only adequate, with Elway at quarterback they usually had no trouble outscoring the opposition.

John's performance in one particular game stood out. On November 4, 1977, the San Fernando Tigers came to Granada Hills with the championship of the

Mid-Valley League up for grabs. It was also the homecoming game for Granada Hills, and hundreds of former players were in attendance.

San Fernando sported one of the most powerful running attacks in California. Over and over again their backs scrambled into and around the Highlanders' defensive line, chewing up the clock and huge chunks of yardage, scoring almost at will.

But Granada Hills had John Elway. Every time it looked as if San Fernando had the game locked up, John brought the Highlanders back, either throwing the ball downfield or scrambling for important yardage.

But with only one minute, 32 seconds left in the game, San Fernando scored to take a 35–32 lead. The game appeared to be over.

After the kickoff, Granada Hills took over on their own 33-yard line. The end zone — and victory — was 67 yards away.

John didn't get nervous. He knew there was still plenty of time to score. When he saw several of his teammates in the huddle looking dejected, he barked, "Hey, let's get it together! We can do this!" John's positive attitude was infectious.

14

The Highlanders worked carefully. Every time John crouched over the center, he looked out at the defense, searching for a weakness. In the Granada offense, John was allowed to "call an audible" or change the play at the line of scrimmage if he wanted to.

Calling an audible on nearly every play, John quickly worked the ball downfield, either hitting his receivers with bullet-like passes or tucking the ball under his arm and picking through the defense himself.

On the sixth play of the drive, he spotted receiver Scott Marshall downfield. He threw a bullet between defenders. Marshall caught the ball before being tripped up at the nine-yard line. There were only 30 seconds left in the game.

Coach Neumeier sent in a play, a pass called an "In and Out" intended for receiver Chris Sutton. It was a timing pass, one of the most difficult passes a quarterback has to make. John had to throw the ball while Sutton was still running and before he made his cut. The ball would have to arrive in the back corner of the end zone at precisely the same time Sutton did. Otherwise, the pass would fail.

Sutton was a fine receiver. He had already caught 11 passes for more than 250 yards.

In the huddle, John called the play and the Highlanders set up at the line. John yelled out the signals and took the ball as Sutton broke downfield.

Sutton drove San Fernando defensive back Larry Maldonado straight downfield. Then, at the goal line, he faked toward the middle, then broke to the back corner of the end zone. Maldonado went for the fake, then spun after Sutton.

Sutton was open and looking for the ball. The ball was already in the air, and it spiraled down perfectly into his hands.

Taking care to keep his feet in bounds, Sutton cradled the ball in his arms. The referee shot both arms into the air. Touchdown Highlanders!

John raced toward the end zone with his teammates and hundreds of fans in celebration. But simultaneously, another referee was waving his hands and blowing his whistle. No one on the Granada Hills team had noticed the yellow penalty marker flying through the air.

The referee called a holding penalty on Granada Hills. Not only did the touchdown not count, but also the line of scrimmage was pushed back another 15 yards, to the 24-yard line.

It took several minutes to stop the celebration and clear the field while the Highlanders crowd booed the referees. As the Highlanders waited for Coach Neumeier to send in another play, Chris Sutton looked over to the sideline and caught the coach's eye.

Neumeier nodded back. Sutton wanted the coach to call the same play. He agreed.

Sutton thought he could get open again. All John Elway had to do was throw another perfect pass. But this time he had to throw it 15 yards farther downfield!

Once more John Elway crouched over the center and took the snap. Sutton took off downfield.

This time, Maldonado was set up several yards deeper. He didn't want the receiver to get past him a second time.

Sutton faked inside but this time Maldonado refused to bite. Sutton had no choice but to break back to the corner of the end zone and hope the ball was there.

He looked up. He saw two things: the ball

dropping from the sky, and Maldonado's hand. The defender hadn't been fooled.

The pass was perfect. Yet Maldonado was able to deflect it with his fingertips. The ball spun crazily in the air. Sutton jumped, turned in the air, and watched it fall into his chest. He pulled it close and thudded to the ground.

As he landed, he heard a tremendous roar. Touchdown!

This time, no penalty marred the celebration. John Elway had thrown a second perfect pass and Chris Sutton had caught it! Granada Hills won, 40–35.

"Even then," said a teammate years later, "you had a sense that if John had the ball, he could make things happen with it. He just had that aura about him." By the end of the season John had passed for more than 3,000 yards, a remarkable figure.

That aura continued on the baseball field the following spring, when John became a standout third baseman. He had major league scouts drooling over his potential. It seemed as if John could do just about anything he put his mind to.

But his mind was still on football. Before John began his senior year in 1978, Coach Neumeier told him that he thought John had a chance to pass for more than 4,000 yards and set a national high school record. When the season began, John set out to prove his coach correct.

For three and a half games, it seemed as if John would not only break the record, but also shatter it. He was averaging nearly 500 passing yards a game!

But in the fourth game of the season, just before halftime, John rolled out to the right and looked downfield for a receiver. Suddenly, he crumpled to the ground. No one had even touched him. His left knee, which he had sprained while playing basketball a few years earlier, had simply given out.

John limped to the sidelines and was taken to the locker room. Jack Elway, who had been watching from the stands, followed.

At halftime, John looked up at his father and told him to tape his knee. Jack warned his son that he thought he was taking an unnecessary risk, but John didn't care. He wanted to play.

He limped through the remainder of the game and lifted his season passing total to 1,837 yards. But it was clear the next day that his knee was badly hurt.

Jack took John to a doctor. The doctor thought John had torn some cartilage and decided to operate. When he opened up John's knee, he discovered more than just torn cartilage. John's anterior cruciate ligament was completely torn.

A ligament is a piece of tissue that holds bone in position. The anterior cruciate ligament, or ACL, winds toward the front of the knee and helps hold the bones of the upper and lower leg in alignment. Without it, the knee joint becomes unstable. For a football player, who is often hit on the legs, the ACL is crucial.

Today, surgical procedures often can repair torn ligaments. But when John hurt his knee, there was little the doctors could do. In 1978, a torn ACL was a career-ending injury for most athletes.

But John wasn't like most athletes. For some reason, even without the ACL, his knee remained stable. Although he couldn't play football for the remainder of the season, one month after the operation, John's doctor examined the knee and, stunned, pronounced John fit enough to begin baseball practice. He even gave John the okay to resume his football career in college the following fall. Even without the ACL, John's knee was stronger than most.

That was important, because fifty-nine colleges nationwide had offered John a football scholarship. More than anything else, he wanted to play college football.

Although John could have gone almost anywhere, he finally chose Stanford University. Just as his father had chosen Granada Hills High School because of its athletic and academic reputation, so too did John select Stanford. Known as the Harvard of the West, Stanford is one of the finest academic schools in the nation. Yet at the same time they have a fine reputation in athletics. The football team, the Cardinals, played a wide-open, professional style that suited John and his passing talents perfectly.

The only possible glitch was that Jack Elway had just been named head coach at San Jose State, an emerging football power. Many observers wondered if SJS had named Elway coach on the assumption that his son would follow him.

But Jack knew that his son had to make his own

decision and never tried to recruit him to San Jose. Besides, both father and son sensed that it was probably a good idea for John to be on his own.

For the remainder of his final year in high school, John threw his energy into baseball. He hit .419 for the season and led his team to the Los Angeles City Championship Game against Crenshaw High.

No one gave Granada Hills much of a chance against Crenshaw, whose lineup included two fabulous players, infielder Chris Brown and outfielder Darryl Strawberry; many considered Strawberry to be the best baseball prospect in the country. Both players later played in the major leagues.

John's team fell behind by one run in the third inning as Crenshaw rocked Granada's starting pitcher. When the Highlanders coach pulled his pitcher, he put John into the game.

Although John had the strongest arm on the team and threw over 90 miles per hour, he rarely pitched. He didn't want to hurt his arm for football, so when he did pitch, he didn't throw curves or change-ups or anything fancy, only fast balls.

That was enough. John gave up only one hit and shut out both Brown and Strawberry. Granada Hills won, 10–4, and John Elway was named Southern California Player of the Year, an award that had previously been won by Hall of Famers Jackie Robinson and Ted Williams.

At the end of the season, the Kansas City Royals major league baseball team selected John in the amateur draft. Although they knew he preferred football, they still tried to persuade him to give professional baseball a try.

Although John was flattered, he had already decided to make football his future. He wanted to play quarterback for the Stanford Cardinals.

For now, anyway.

Chapter Three:
1979–1982

From the Cardinals to the Yankees

When John arrived on the campus of Stanford University for the beginning of his freshman year of college, he had an immediate impact. Because of John, several players quit the football team!

As one of Stanford's best known recruits, John was well-known to the other players on the team. Already, some members of the press were touting him as an eventual Heisman Trophy candidate, the award given annually to the best player in college football.

But when football practice started, such predictions didn't matter. As John already knew, his performance on the filed was all that counted.

Senior quarterback Turk Schonert was already firmly installed as Stanford's starting quarterback. He was a star, and would later go on to have an effective career in the NFL as quarterback of the Cincinnati Bengals.

But there were several other quarterbacks waiting in the wings to take Schonert's place. Like Elway, both Babe Laufenberg and Grayson Rogers had been heavily recruited in high school and had entered Stanford with great expectations. As underclassmen, they had bided their time behind Schonert and expected to battle each other for the starter's job after the 1979 season.

But when John Elway showed up, Laufenberg and Rogers saw the writing on the wall. Although only a freshman, Elway was already Schonert's heir apparent. Both quarterbacks knew the freshman already possessed a much stronger arm, was more mobile, and understood the offense as well as they did.

So Laufenberg and Rogers quit the team and transferred to other schools, Laufenberg to Indiana and Rogers to the University of the Pacific. Each went on to standout collegiate careers and eventually received opportunities to play professional football.

Meanwhile, John Elway played caddy to Schonert and tried to adjust to college life.

Athletes get little special treatment at Stanford. They are expected to take the same grueling academic schedule as the other students and still find time for practice, games, and other activities required by their sport.

This fact often puts the Stanford football team at a disadvantage against other schools. Many high school players who are fine football players simply don't qualify for Stanford's rigorous academic program. Stanford therefore often lacked the depth of other teams. As a member of one of the nation's premier college football leagues, the Pacific Coast Conference, or what was then called the Pac-10 (now the Pac-12), the Cardinals sometimes had a hard time competing.

Although John had little trouble adjusting to college, he still found that it was a challenge to budget his time. It seemed as if every moment was either spent on the football field, in class, or studying.

The Cardinals played well behind Schonert in 1979, but fell well short of a championship and failed to qualify for a postseason bowl game. Schonert got the bulk of the playing time, but John made appearances in nine games and did nothing to lower the expectations of the coaching staff.

That spring, he even played outfield on the college baseball team. After being the center of attention on the football team, he enjoyed being just another member of the baseball team. He hit .269, a good start for a freshman.

As a sophomore, John took over the reins of the potent Cardinals' offense. It was good that he did, for the youthful Cardinals' defense wasn't up to the task of shutting down the opposition's offense. John would pass and run the team in for a touchdown, only to watch helplessly as the defense gave up points as fast as he could score them. It was frustrating not to win very often, but at the same time John received plenty of opportunities to display his talent.

Then one game, everything came together. No one gave the Cardinals a prayer against powerful Oklahoma, one of the best teams in the country. But for once, the defense came through. John turned in a vintage performance, passing at will and running circles around the highly regarded Oklahoma defense. After the game, Oklahoma coaching legend

Barry Switzer said that John put on "the greatest exhibition of quarterback play and passing I've ever seen."

He ended the season by setting a host of Pac-10 records, including most touchdown passes, completions, and total offense. He also set the single-game record for touchdown passes when he exploded for six against Oregon. His performance earned him All-American honors.

John followed his spectacular play on the football field with equally good work on the baseball diamond. He hit .361 and knocked in 50 runs in only 49 games. He helped lead the Cardinals into the NCAA Central regional tournament, where he was a unanimous choice for the all-tournament team.

Pro-baseball scouts were impressed, but most shied away from drafting him, as they assumed that Elway was looking toward pro football, not pro baseball, for his future employment. But the New York Yankees weren't like most other teams. Their brash, free-spending owner George Steinbrenner was intrigued by the scouting reports on Elway and well aware of the publicity he would attract by signing Elway to a baseball contract.

In the draft after the baseball season, the Yankees picked Elway in the second round; he was the fifty-fourth player selected in the entire country. They intended to sign him to a contract. Steinbrenner knew it would be a real coup if the Yankees could persuade Elway to turn his back on football.

Before 1974, it had been impossible for an athlete to play professionally in one sport and on the collegiate level in another. But in 1974, the NCAA, the organization that controls college athletics, decided they were losing too many multisport athletes to professional teams. So they changed the rules to make it possible for a player to do both.

John and the Yankees eventually agreed to a contract worth $150,000. Although John would be ineligible to play baseball for the Cardinals as a junior, he agreed to give pro baseball a try after his senior year.

By the beginning of John's junior year, expectations were high. The defense appeared to have matured, and with Elway directing the offense, the Cardinals seemed ready to compete with any team in the country. Some prognosticators were even predicting a Pac-10 championship and an appearance in the Rose Bowl by the Cardinals. That was just what John had in mind.

But the squad was saddled with a grueling schedule. They played well early in the season, but then lost several games by fewer than ten points. The opposition knew that to beat Stanford, all they had to do was key on Elway. Almost every game, he faced a nonstop pass rush and innumerable blitzes.

Yet John usually held his own. Far more maneuverable and faster than other quarterbacks, he was developing the ability to make something out of nothing on almost every play. In fact, it often appeared as if he were at his most dangerous when he was flushed from the pocket and forced to scramble.

Such situations put all his talents on display. As the defense charged around him, John would dance from the pocket, roll out, duck one tackler and dodge another, and then, while sprinting with half the defense in pursuit, somehow throw a bullet far downfield. He was the most exciting player in the country.

But the long season took a toll on John. Every week, he got a little more banged up, spraining an ankle one week, chipping a bone in his left hand in another, and suffering a concussion.

One game was particularly brutal. John had to play against his father's team, San Jose State.

Going into the game, he was already hurting. Meanwhile, San Jose's defense was fired up and wanted to impress their coach. The Cardinals' running attack was nonexistent that day. For 60 long minutes it appeared that all John did was run around the backfield, throw a hurried pass, and then get knocked to the ground.

San Jose State won, 28–6, but it was a bittersweet win for Jack Elway. John played the worst game of his collegiate career, completing only 6 of 24 passes for 72 yards. He threw five interceptions and was sacked seven times. Each time Jack Elway's team slammed his son to the ground, he grimaced as if feeling the pain himself.

Stanford finished the season a disappointing 4–7, their worst record in years. John slumped from his remarkable performance the year before, although he still managed to throw for more than 2,500 yards and 20 touchdowns. Yet pro football scouts weren't put off. If anything, they were even more impressed by his toughness.

At six foot three and 200 pounds, Elway was an NFL scout's dream. He was fast and mobile enough to escape the pass rush and he had the best arm of any quarterback in the country, pro or college. Furthermore, the coach's son knew how to read a defense and make the correct decision with the football. The summer before his senior year, he was the most ballyhooed player in college, a candidate for the Heisman Trophy and the likely first pick in the NFL draft the following spring.

But before John could focus on football again, he had to fulfill his obligation to the Yankees. As soon as his junior year ended, in May 1982, he joined the Yankees minor league team in Oneonta, New York.

Oneonta competed in the New York–Pennsylvania League, a Class A minor league that was meant for younger players in their first year or two of professional baseball. While some Yankees officials wanted John to start at a higher classification, the Yankees wanted to give him a chance to succeed right away. They were afraid that if he failed, he'd quit baseball for good.

The life of a minor league baseball player was a step down from the life of a Stanford Cardinal. At Stanford, everything was first class, from the locker room and stadium all the way to the planes the team traveled on and the hotels they stayed in on the road.

At Oneonta, John shared a small apartment with several teammates, dressed in a tiny locker room, traveled to games on a cramped bus, and stayed in cheap motels. But he loved it, maybe because on the baseball field, no one was expecting him to win every game, and no one was chasing him around trying to knock him down. He was just another guy trying to learn to play ball.

At first, John was overwhelmed by the competition. Every pitcher in the minor leagues had been the best pitcher on their high school or college team. They threw hard and had much better control than John was accustomed to facing in the Pac-10.

He played right field, where his powerful arm could dissuade base runners from taking an extra base. The Yankees immediately installed the left-handed swinger in the third or fourth spot in the batting order, the most important place in the lineup.

Yet in his first nineteen at-bats, John got only one hit.

For some players, such a poor start would have destroyed their confidence and driven them from the game. But not John. Although he wasn't accustomed to failure, he had plenty of experience in coming back after a rough start. He stayed focused and soon began to display his prowess as a ballplayer.

During the next two months John hit .348, with 5 home runs, 2 triples, 6 doubles, 25 RBIs, 28 walks, and 13 stolen bases. John's teammates and the Yankees were impressed.

As one scout later recalled, "He could do it all. John was as close as you could come to being a 'can't miss' prospect."

Teammate Tim Birtsas, a pitcher who later made it to the major leagues, agreed. "You had to be impressed with his talent," he says. "But what impressed me the most was that he was so down-to-earth."

Yet despite his success, as summer began to give way to fall, John's thoughts returned to the gridiron. As planned, he left the team in August and reported to Stanford to begin his final year of college football. The Yankees retained possession of his baseball contract, however, and hoped that John would consider a return to the game after college.

In his last season at Stanford, John continued to impress his admirers who thought football was his best sport. Among other achievements, he led the Cardinals to a surprising win over Washington, then the number-one ranked team in the country. He also led the nation in touchdown passes. For the first time in his collegiate career, it looked as if John Elway was going to a Bowl game.

In order to make a Bowl appearance, all the Cardinals had to do was defeat their arch rival, the University of California, in the last game of the regular season. Officials for the Hall of Fame Bowl had already announced that if Stanford won they intended to extend an invitation to the Bowl game.

When Stanford plays Cal, the press and fans simply refer to it as the Big Game. And John had already proven there was no better player in the country in a big game than John Elway. Stanford was a heavy favorite, and a nationwide television audience tuned in to watch Elway do something unforgettable. He was memorable, all right, but in a way that they hadn't imagined. The final outcome of the Big Game came to symbolize Elway's years at Stanford. For although it was exciting, it was, for Stanford fans, ultimately disappointing.

Cal played perhaps its best game of the season, and led 19–17 with only one minute, 27 seconds left to play. The Cardinals took over on their own 20-yard line.

On first down, Stanford tried a swing pass, and John flipped the ball to a running back sweeping out of the backfield. The back caught the ball, but Cal was ready. The back reversed field and tried to dodge and dart away, but was finally pulled to the ground for a 17-yard loss. Then, on second and third downs, Elway threw incompletions.

John's back was against the wall. It was fourth down and twenty-seven.

Eight Cal defenders dropped into pass coverage while three linemen tried to pressure John. But he stayed calm and at the last moment drilled a rocket to receiver Emile Harry for a 29-yard gain. The Cardinals were still alive!

Elway moved the team downfield, then Stanford crossed up Cal with a sweep play that gained 21 yards and put them within field goal range. With four seconds to go Mark Harmon calmly booted a field goal. Stanford led, 20–19.

All the Cardinals had to do was kick the ball downfield and make a tackle. To prevent Cal from setting up a long run back, the Cardinal coaching staff ordered their kicker to make a squib kick, a kick that bounces slowly along the ground and is virtually impossible to run back for a touchdown.

The kicker did as he was told and squibbed the ball downfield, where it was picked up on the California 43-yard line by the Bears' Kevin Moen. The Stanford kicking team swarmed toward him and seemed to make the tackle. But at the last instant Moen lateraled the ball to another California player.

As he did, the California players began to walk onto the field to congratulate their rivals, and the Stanford marching band, massed in the Stanford end zone, began to take the field for their postgame performance.

But the game wasn't over yet. The Cal player who had taken the lateral ran, and just as he was being tackled, lateraled again.

A third player took off with the ball, weaving through the defense. Before he could be stopped, he lateraled the ball a fourth time.

Yet another Cal player took off with the ball. He was tackled, but before his knee touched the ground, he threw a blind lateral into the air behind him.

By this time, Kevin Moen, who had originally fielded the squib kick, had gotten back up and followed the play down the field. He plucked the ball from the air and took off downfield once more, weaving his way between confused players and overzealous members of the band who had marched onto the field!

He burst into the end zone through a trombone player, who went hurtling through the air and landed flat on his back! An official hesitated, looked around, then raised his hands in the air. Touchdown!

The Stanford coaching staff and several players argued in vain to try to get the officials to reverse their call — after all, the field was blocked by the band and dozens of Cal players who had walked onto the field — but they refused. The touchdown stood. Stanford lost.

There would be no Bowl game for John Elway. His college career was over.

Chapter Four:
1982–1983

Rookie

During the few months following his last college football game, Elway tried to focus on finishing his undergraduate degree in economics and enjoying his final days as a college student. He lived in a small room on the upper floor of a frat house and enjoyed spending time with his buddies, who treated him like any other member of the fraternity. John also spent a lot of time with his girlfriend, Janet, who was a nationally ranked swimmer and competed on the swim team at Stanford. They spent hours together as John pondered his future.

It was a foregone conclusion that John would be the first pick in the upcoming NFL draft in the spring of 1983. Although he had finished second to Georgia running back Herschel Walker in Heisman Trophy balloting, Walker still had another year remaining in college. Elway was easily the best player available in the draft.

The NFL had just completed a disappointing year that had been marred by a player strike and that had been limited to only nine regular season games. Fans, owners, and players alike were tired of football discussions that degenerated into arguments about money. Everyone looked optimistically toward the 1983 season.

Everyone, that is, but John Elway. The Baltimore Colts, who had finished the 1982 season with a dismal record of no wins, eight losses, and one tie, owned the rights to the first pick in the NFL draft. They were in desperate need of a quarterback and announced their plan to select Elway with the first pick.

Although John was flattered that the Colts thought so highly of him, their announcement didn't make him happy. There was no way John Elway wanted to play for the Baltimore Colts.

One reason was the Colts' offense. They played an unimaginative, plodding, ball-control style of offense that Elway hated. He was much more comfortable in a wide-open passing attack.

Another reason was the Colts' offensive line. They were young and inexperienced. If he played for the Colts, John knew he'd spend most of his rookie season running for his life.

Coach Frank Kush was yet another reason. Kush had been hired by Baltimore owner Robert Irsay in 1982 and given the charge to turn around the once-proud franchise. He was a tough disciplinarian who approached each game and practice as if it were a military battle. Although he had been successful as a college coach, older, more experienced, and more mature professional players detested his overbearing style. If given a choice, no one in the league wanted to play for Kush.

Colts owner Robert Irsay provided John with one more reason not to play for Baltimore. When Elway told a reporter that he would prefer to play on the West Coast, Irsay branded him as immature and selfish. His comments made Elway even more determined to play elsewhere.

Elway's contract with the Yankees gave him some leverage. He intimated that if it came down to a decision to play for the Colts or play pro baseball, he might just play baseball. "I can be happy either way," he told *Sports Illustrated.* "I won't look back."

Nonetheless, on April 26, 1983, draft day, the Colts selected Elway. He showed his displeasure by refusing to accept a congratulatory phone call from Irsay and telling his agent not to negotiate with the team.

Irsay was infuriated, and continued to blast Elway. Frustrated and angry Baltimore fans echoed Irsay's comments and sent thousands of hate letters to Elway. Any remote chance that Elway might change his mind was drowned out by their vocal criticism.

The Colts finally threw up their hands and began to entertain offers for Elway from other NFL teams. After sorting through several bids, on May 4 they traded him to the Denver Broncos in exchange for offensive lineman Chris Hinton, a number-one draft pick in 1984, backup quarterback Mark Hermann, and one million dollars.

Elway had gotten what he wanted, but it came at a price. Although he quickly signed a five-year contract with Denver worth five million dollars — the biggest contract for any player in the league at the time — his unique holdout left him branded as a selfish player who thought only about himself. Veteran players were particularly put off.

John arrived at Bronco training camp in Greeley, Colorado in late July of 1983 under tremendous pressure to live up to his five-million-dollar contract. After the Broncos reached the Super Bowl in 1978, at which they lost to Dallas 27–10, they had fallen on hard times. In 1982, coach Dan Reeves's club had finished 2–7. Broncos fans and the Denver organization looked to John as a savior.

The press watched every move he made. Only one other pro sports team, the NBA Denver Nuggets, was located in the city. But the Broncos were far more popular. Their fans lived and died with every game. As their most visible player, John Elway was under a magnifying glass from the first day he stepped on the field. Thousands of fans turned out at every practice.

Most NFL rookies have a difficult time gaining the respect of their peers, but the Broncos veterans were doubly hard on Elway. They resented not only his holdout but his huge contract. Veteran quarterback Steve DeBerg was popular with his teammates, and many Broncos didn't like the fact that the team had acquired another quarterback.

In the locker room, the vets all but ignored Elway. On the field, they did their best to make his life miserable, knocking him to the ground at every opportunity.

As if all that wasn't bad enough, John had to try to learn an entirely new offense. In only a few weeks of camp, he was expected to memorize nearly one hundred plays, each of which had several variations. Math classes at Stanford had been much easier.

Like most rookie quarterbacks, Elway initially struggled in practice, where he split time with De-Berg and backup Gary Kubiak. Observers weren't impressed, and began to wonder if Elway was going to turn out to be a bust. Many college quarterbacks even more accomplished than Elway had failed to make it in professional football.

That perception changed when the Broncos played their first preseason game versus the Seattle Seahawks at Denver's Mile High Stadium before eighty thousand screaming fans.

Elway entered the game in the fourth quarter. Just a few plays into his career, he zipped a long pass to receiver Steve Watson, sending the crowd into hysterics. That was the player they had expected to see! A few plays later he threaded a pass between two defenders to Rick Upchurch at the two-yard line. Running back Sammy Winder then powered in for a touchdown. In his first series, Elway had led Denver to a touchdown.

After only a few exhibition games, Denver coach Dan Reeves named Elway the starting quarterback. John responded by playing like a rookie.

In the season opener against Pittsburgh, the Steelers' vaunted defense went after Elway with a vengeance. It seemed they shared the Broncos' feelings of animosity against the young highly paid star.

The first three times the Broncos had the ball, Elway failed to complete a pass as Pittsburgh forced him to rush every play. The fourth time Denver got the ball, John finally completed a pass, but it was an interception by Pittsburgh. The next time, he was sacked, and later he fumbled while being sacked again.

Mercifully, Reeves removed him from the game. Elway watched dejectedly from the sidelines as De-Berg led the team to a 14–10 win. But a week later, when Denver traveled to Baltimore, Elway was back in the starting lineup.

Baltimore fans and players had circled the date on their calendar weeks before. They promised to give Elway an unforgettable reception.

He was booed long and loud from the moment he took the field, and the fired-up Colts teed off on the increasingly nervous rookie. After completing a mere 9 of 21 passes for just over 100 yards, Elway was yanked from the game. DeBerg calmly led the Broncos to their second win. All John could say afterward was, "I'm bewildered. It hasn't been much fun so far."

To be fair, he wasn't playing quite as badly as it seemed. The Denver offensive line was doing a poor job, and Elway was still learning the offense. But at the same time, the five-million-dollar man was playing far below the expectations of his salary.

Elway showed little improvement over the next two weeks. The Broncos lost twice, and finally, late in the fifth game of the season, a 31–14 loss to Chicago, Reeves benched Elway and made DeBerg the starter. The Broncos responded by winning the next four games.

Then DeBerg hurt his shoulder and Elway was pressed into service once again. He played better, and even extracted a measure of revenge against Baltimore by throwing three touchdown passes in the final 10 minutes to give the Broncos a 21–19 win. But he was still maddeningly inconsistent. When DeBerg had recovered, Elway went back to the bench. Although the Broncos qualified for the playoffs, they lost to Seattle 31–7 in the first round. Elway appeared in the game in a mop-up role.

Elway was relieved that the season was finally over, and he returned to California. He and Janet were married, and Elway returned to his alma mater to help his father, who had been named head coach at Stanford. He pondered everything that had happened, and wondered how someone at the age of twenty-three could already feel so old.

All he wanted to do was forget his first season of professional football. But at the same time, he realized he had nowhere to go but up.

Chapter Five:
1984–1985

The Starter

In the off-season, the Broncos decided it was time to make some changes. Although DeBerg had played well at quarterback, he had limited talent and couldn't throw the ball deep. Also, they didn't want to repeat the quarterback controversy that had dogged the team in the 1983–1984 season.

The Broncos traded DeBerg to the Tampa Bay Buccaneers and handed the starting job to Elway. To help him along, they hired assistant coach Mike Shanahan to help retool the Denver offense.

Head coach Dan Reeves, although not as conservative as Frank Kush, was a traditionalist. He believed that in order to win, a team had to run the football first and play good defense. When they did pass the ball, he expected his quarterback to stay in the pocket and throw to his wide receivers. Running backs were rarely sent out into the pass routes.

But there were a few problems with Reeves's approach. The offense was predictable and Denver lacked the physically dominant players required to carry out Reeves's philosophy. The offense line was small, and the defense, while adequate, wasn't very physical.

Besides, professional football was undergoing a transition. Rule changes and tactical advances began to favor the passing game.

Despite the potential problems Reeves's coaching strategies presented, John was determined to succeed. After the pounding he took in 1983, he worked out hard in the off-season and arrived at training camp with an additional fifteen pounds of muscle.

The DeBerg trade and the presence of Shanahan made him feel more confident. His teammates began to accept him and Shanahan lobbied Reeves to make the forward pass more prominent in the Denver offense. He believed that if the offense took advantage of Elway's strengths, it would be far more effective.

Elway opened the 1984 season much more relaxed. In an effort to help him regain his confidence, Reeves had decreased the number of plays he had to learn. This time, he was determined to bring Elway along more slowly.

The strategy worked, not just for Elway, but for the entire offense. Everyone was more comfortable. Running back Sammy Winder gave the team its first consistent running game in years, and Elway finally started to play to his potential. He wasn't the best quarterback in the league, but he was far from the worst.

The Broncos opened the season by winning eight of their first nine games. They weren't crushing the opposition or playing very exciting football, but they were winning.

Then, in the tenth week of the season, the Broncos played host to the New England Patriots. With only minutes left to play, the game was tied, 19–19. Thus far the Patriots, although not a particularly good defensive team, had stifled the Denver offense. Every team in the league was starting to figure out that the Broncos would run on first and second downs and pass only when they needed to on third down. It was easy to play defense if you knew in advance what the opposition was likely to do.

With the outcome of the game in balance, the Broncos went to their two-minute offense. The two-minute offense is a desperate strategy in which a team usually abandons the running game entirely and passes the ball downfield as fast as possible. Often, the team doesn't even have a running back on the field, but uses an extra wide receiver instead.

That was the way John Elway was meant to play the game. As he stood over the center and barked out the signals, he scanned New England's defense and called an audible.

The Patriots were in the "prevent" defense, a strategy that protects against the long pass. It works, but usually leaves receivers open on shorter pass routes and gives the quarterback plenty of time to throw the ball.

Elway took the ball from the center, dropped back, and looked downfield. He deftly side-stepped a rushing lineman and rolled out to his right, while directing his receivers with a wave of his hand. It was sandlot football orchestrated by a master.

He spotted an open receiver and threw a perfect pass. Complete! The Broncos were on the move.

Seven more times on the drive Elway calmly dropped back and picked the New England defense apart. In just over two minutes he drove the Broncos in for a last-second touchdown. Denver won, 26–19.

One week later, against San Diego, Elway faced a similar situation. The Chargers were leading 13–9 late in the game when the Broncos once again went to their two-minute offense.

In that situation, Elway was the most dangerous player in football. In nine spectacular, heart-stopping plays he moved the team down to the one-yard line, then handed the ball to Sammy Winder. Winder plunged in for the game-winning score. Then, in the next-to-the-last game of the season, Elway repeated that same comeback when he engineered another last-second drive against San Diego to win again.

Suddenly John Elway was the most talked-about player in the league, and the Broncos were the most-improved team in football. They won the

Western Division of the American Football Conference and qualified for the playoffs with a 13–3
record. Although the Steelers snuffed out the Broncos' Super Bowl dreams in the first round of the
playoffs, for the first time in his NFL career John
Elway knew he belonged. He finished the season
with 18 touchdown passes and 56 percent of his
passes completed.

In the off-season Mike Shanahan was promoted
from receivers' coach to offensive coordinator, a
move that Elway wholeheartedly supported. Now
that Elway had a taste of success, he wanted more,
and he thought Shanahan could help.

But in 1985, not everything went as planned. The
Broncos were hit with a series of injuries that weak-
ened the defense and destroyed much of the offensive line. All of a sudden, they couldn't run the ball
or keep the other team from scoring.

All they had was John Elway. Often, that was just
enough to win.

He became a veritable one-man team, throwing
the football forty or fifty times a game or tucking it
under his arm and weaving his way down the field.

Elway scrambles with the ball to put the Broncos ahead of the
Cleveland Browns in the 1989 AFC Championship Game.

John Elway rears back to catapult a 56-yard touchdown pass in Super Bowl XXII against the Washington Redskins in 1988.

Elway is one step ahead of an Oakland Raider, moving the ball for 9 yards.

A portrait of concentration, Elway prepares to deliver a touchdown bomb against the Kansas City Chiefs.

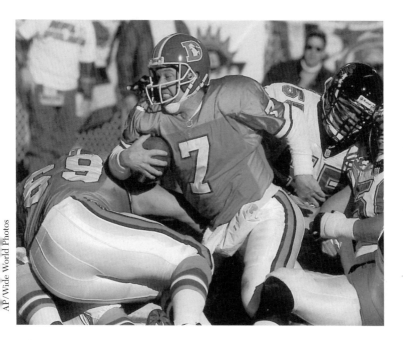

John Elway tries to power through the Jacksonville Jaguars' defense.

With the AFC championship on the line, Elway looks to
complete a pass against the Pittsburgh Steelers.

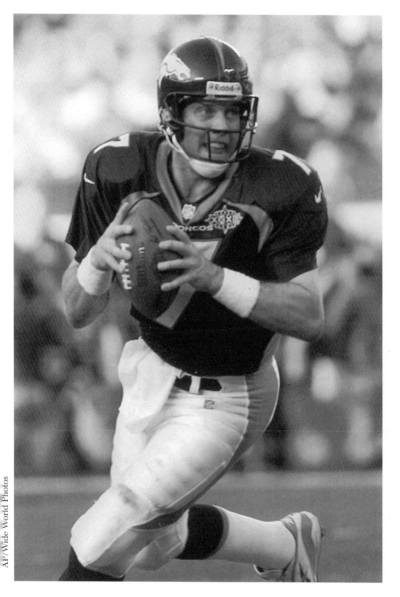

A super scramble during the first half of Super Bowl XXXII against the Green Bay Packers.

The winning quarterback of Super Bowl XXXII!

Elway celebrates with Broncos head coach and longtime friend
Mike Shanahan.

A peaceful moment months after the Super Bowl, with wife Janet, daughter Juliana, and son Jack.

John Elway's Career Highlights

1985:
Led the NFL single-season record for attempts (605), total rushing and
  passing plays (656), and total offense (4,414)

1986:
Led Broncos to first AFC championship in nine years
Earned a spot in the Pro Bowl
Awarded Seattle Gold Helmet (Professional Football Player of the Year)
Honorable mention All-NFL and All-AFC

1987:
NFL MVP
Led Broncos to second AFC championship, the first quarterback to do so
  since 1978–1979
Led Broncos to Super Bowl XXII
Became first quarterback in Super Bowl history to catch a pass
All-NFL, All-AFC, AFC Player of the Year, AFC Offensive Player of
  the Year

1989:
Led Broncos to third AFC championship
Led Broncos to Super Bowl XXIV

1993:
AFC MVP
AFC Offensive Player of the Year
AFC Player of the Year

1994:
Earned a spot in the Pro Bowl

1995:
Led AFC in passing yards

1996:
Led AFC in quarterback rating
Became second quarterback in NFL history to throw for more than 40,000
  yards and rush for more than 3,000 yards
Became winningest quarterback in NFL history with a total of 126 regular-
  season wins
Earned a spot in the Pro Bowl

(continued on next page)

1997:
Led the Broncos to victory in Super Bowl XXXII
Recipient of the NFL Players Association Mackey Award for top quarterback
  in the AFC

Notable achievement:
For seven consecutive seasons (1985–1991), passed for more than 3,000
  yards and rushed for more than 200 yards, a record that may never be broken

John Elway's Professional Career Stats

Year	Attempts	Completions	Completions' Percentage	Yards	Touchdowns	Interceptions
1983	259	123	47.5	1663	7	14
1984	380	214	56.3	2598	18	15
1985	605	327	54.0	3891	22	23
1986	504	280	55.6	3485	19	13
1987	410	224	54.6	3198	19	12
1988	496	274	55.2	3309	17	19
1989	416	223	53.6	3051	18	18
1990	502	294	58.6	3526	15	14
1991	451	242	53.7	3253	13	12
1992	316	174	55.1	2242	10	17
1993	551	348	63.2	4030	25	10
1994	494	307	62.1	3490	16	10
1995	542	316	58.3	3970	26	14
1996	466	287	61.6	3328	26	14
1997	502	280	55.8	3635	27	11
Pro Totals (15 Years)	**6894**	**3913**	**56.8**	**48,669**	**278**	**216**

On five separate occasions, he led the Broncos to a fourth-quarter comeback.

Denver fans loved his style of play, but Coach Dan Reeves didn't like to see Elway trying to do it all, even when he had no choice. The two often clashed, sometimes even in the middle of a game. Reeves questioned Elway's use of audibles and his decisions about passing. Before long, there was genuine dislike between the two men, and they rarely talked.

Late in the season, the Broncos seemed bound for the playoffs, only to lose two overtime contests to finish with an 11–5 record. The losses cost the Broncos a division title, and in a complicated series of tiebreakers, they became the first team to finish 11–5 and fail to make the playoffs.

John's numbers at the end of the year were staggering. With 605 pass attempts, he narrowly missed breaking the NFL record of 609 held by Dan Fouts. He led the league in total offense, and his 327 completions and 3,891 passing yards were second in the league.

While John was happy with his individual performance, he was dissatisfied with the way the Broncos finished the season. Despite all the comebacks, the team hadn't reached their goal of making the play-offs. Elway knew he wouldn't be considered a great player until he showed that he could lead his team to the Super Bowl. As he entered the 1986 season, that was his goal.

Chapter Six:
1986

The Drive

Elway began the 1986 campaign playing even better than he had the year before. As a team, the Broncos had improved little. Their defense was still suspect while the offensive line continued to have trouble blocking well enough to support a consistent running attack. Only John Elway continued to improve.

Despite the fact that opposing teams were now keying on Elway on virtually every play, he continued to wreak havoc. Though they knew John was going to pass the ball on almost every play, they were almost powerless to stop him.

The Broncos jumped out and won six games before losing to the New York Jets, 22–10. They played .500 football the rest of the season, giving up 136 points over their last four games as the defense almost totally collapsed. Still, the Broncos held on to finish 11–5 and win the division title by a game, ahead of Kansas City and Seattle.

In the first round of the playoffs, the Broncos faced the New England Patriots in Denver. Elway knew that it was time to prove he was capable of leading his team to the Super Bowl.

It was a tough, hard-fought contest. And although Elway's passes were often off-target, he found another way to win.

In the second quarter, with Denver nursing a slim, 3–0 lead, Elway had the ball on the 22-yard line. He dropped back to pass, but couldn't find an open receiver.

Instead of panicking and either taking a sack or throwing the ball out of bounds, Elway turned himself into a running back. He darted upfield between the startled New England defense and burst into the end zone for a touchdown. The extra-point kick was good and Denver led, 10–0.

Energized by his performance, the Denver offensive line responded by playing its best game of the season. Sammy Winder ran for over 100 yards. Elway, despite completing only 13 passes for the game, made each one count as he threw for a total of

257 yards. Denver controlled the ball for nearly the entire game for a 22–17 victory.

The win earned the team the right to play the Cleveland Browns for the AFC championship. The winner would go to the Super Bowl.

The Broncos had to travel to Cleveland for the game. Cleveland's Municipal Stadium had a well-deserved reputation as a very tough place to play. Located on the shores of Lake Erie, the aging, cavernous stadium was usually packed with 80,000 rabid Browns fans. In one end zone, known as the Dog Pound, Cleveland's most rambunctious fans kept up a racket that lasted the whole game. They intimidated many teams with antics that included wearing dog masks and throwing dog bones onto the field.

Few observers gave the Broncos much of a chance to win. Elway turned up with a sore ankle, and despite their performance the week before, the Broncos' defense was still suspect. And Cleveland quarterback Bernie Kosar was hot! The week before he had thrown for nearly 500 yards in Cleveland's victory over the New York Jets.

It was cold and gray in Cleveland on the day of

the game, and a bone-chilling thirty-mile-per-hour wind was blowing off the lake into the stadium.

Both teams had a hard time playing well under such trying conditions. When either Elway or Kosar put the ball into the air, the swirling wind often sent it on a wild trajectory. The slick, muddy turf made traction difficult for the runners.

Although Denver led early, in the fourth quarter the Browns pushed for two scores and took a 20–13 lead. The Broncos fumbled the kickoff after Cleveland's final score, but luckily fell on the ball on their own two-yard line. With less than five minutes to play the Broncos had to move the ball 98 yards for a touchdown.

As Elway entered the huddle, one of his teammates looked at him and quipped, "We've got 'em just where we want 'em," in reference to Elway's ability to lead a last-minute comeback. Elway smiled, then got to work.

At first, the Broncos played conservatively. Elway hit Sammy Winder for a five-yard gain on a swing pass. Then Winder ran for three more yards, setting up third down. Winder narrowly made a first down with another run.

Now the Broncos had a little room to move. After another short run by Winder, Elway dropped back to pass. But when he saw that his receivers were covered, he started to scramble. Despite his sore ankle, he scampered for an 11-yard gain and a first down.

Only three minutes remained in the game. The Broncos had to hurry.

On the next two plays Elway threw complete passes of 22 and 12 yards to move the ball into Cleveland territory.

But after the two-minute warning, the Browns' defense stiffened. Elway threw an incompletion and then was sacked for an eight-yard loss.

It was third and eighteen, now-or-never time for the Broncos.

Elway lined up in the shotgun formation several yards behind the line of scrimmage. The Cleveland fans cheered and roared as loudly as they could. It was impossible to hear the signals, so the Broncos decided to go on a silent count. But the center botched the play and made a poor snap. The ball squirted back low to the ground.

Elway calmly scooped it up as if it were a soft

line-drive hit to the outfield, then drilled a 20-yard completion to receiver Mark Jackson. First down. The Broncos were still alive!

The Dog Pound turned silent. Cleveland fans started to get nervous.

On the next play, the Broncos gained 11 yards on a screen pass. Then Elway threw another short pass to the sidelines to stop the clock. There was just over a minute left to play.

On second down, Elway went back to pass, then saw an opening and made a quick decision. He eluded a tackler and cut upfield, sliding down at the five-yard line.

Time was running out. At the back of the end zone, the Dog Pound was in a fury. Dog bones rained from the sky.

Elway dropped back again. He knew the wind was at its strongest in the end zone. He would have to throw the ball hard and throw it perfectly.

He spotted Mark Jackson cutting across the back of the end zone and anticipated a narrow opening between defenders closing from each direction. Then he wound up like a pitcher and threw his best fastball.

Zip! The ball cut through the air as if shot from a gun. Jackson pulled it from the air for a touchdown. The Dog Pound started whimpering.

Kicker Rich Karlis's extra point tied the game and moments later the final whistle blew. The game was headed to overtime!

The Broncos won the coin toss and received the kick. The disheartened Browns tried to dig in.

But Elway couldn't be stopped. He threw two long passes and moved the Broncos to within field goal range. Karlis calmly drilled the 33-yard kick, and the game was over. Denver won, 23–20!

Elway limped off the field as happy and exhausted as he had ever been in his life. His uniform was smeared with mud and splattered with blood, but he didn't care. The Broncos were going to the Super Bowl.

Everyone who saw the game was certain they had seen the emergence of one of the greatest quarterbacks to ever play football. In the worst possible conditions, Elway's rocket arm, running ability, and unmatched leadership had turned almost certain defeat into victory.

After the game, observers were effusive in their

praise. Philadelphia Eagles coach Buddy Ryan said, "He's got the mobility of Fran Tarkenton and the arm of Joe Namath," in reference to two Hall of Fame quarterbacks. Former Denver quarterback Craig Morton concurred, saying, "He's the only quarterback I've ever seen who could have pulled that off."

John was happy but humble. "You gotta get lucky," he said. "You gotta keep a positive attitude. If you think you can get it done, you figure out a way to get it done."

Now all Elway had to do was figure out a way to get it done in the biggest football game of the season — the Super Bowl.

Chapter Seven:

1987–1988

Super Busts

In Super Bowl XXI, on January 25, 1987, John Elway seemed poised for greatness. A Super Bowl win would confirm his place as one of the greatest quarterbacks ever.

He was superconfident. At a pregame rally held in Denver, he told a crowd of 63,000 fans, "If you thought last week was good, wait until next week."

The Broncos were matched against the National Football Conference champion, the New York Giants. Led by coach Bill Parcells and quarterback Phil Simms, the Giants had finished the season with a league best 14–2 record. They had embarrassed the San Francisco 49ers 44–3 in the first round of the playoffs and shut out the Washington Redskins 17–0 in the NFC championship game. They were heavy favorites.

But when John Elway was on the field, the Broncos always had a chance. Elway was looking forward to the game more than any he had ever played. The setting was going to be the Rose Bowl, in Pasadena, near Granada Hills, where Elway grew up. Furthermore, the Rose Bowl game was a collegiate goal that had eluded Elway. It seemed the perfect place to prove himself a champion quarterback.

With more than 100,000 fans in attendance and millions more watching on television, the game began as if made to order for the Broncos. Denver took the opening kickoff. Elway smartly marched the team into Giants territory, where Rich Karlis boomed a 48-yard field goal to put Denver ahead.

But New York quarterback Phil Simms came right back at the Broncos. He led New York on a 78-yard touchdown drive to take the lead.

Not to be outdone, Elway responded by making a series of crisp passes and driving the Broncos down the field again. Then, from the four-yard line, he improvised on a broken play and bulled his way into the end zone. The first quarter ended with Denver in the lead, 10–7.

The Broncos got the ball back early in the second quarter. Elway was at the top of his game and gave the New York defense fits. He hit receiver Vance Johnson for a 58-yard completion, and soon the Broncos had a first down on the New York one-yard line. They seemed certain to score.

On the first play, Elway rolled out and looked to pass, but couldn't find a receiver. He was sacked for a one-yard loss.

Now Denver got conservative. Dan Reeves didn't like putting the ball into the air so close to the goal line, and after Elway's failure on first down, he abandoned the strategy. Even though the Broncos had had trouble running the ball all year, and although Elway was picking apart the New York defense, Reeves chose to run the ball.

Two running plays pushed the Broncos back to the six-yard line. Rich Karlis came on to try a field goal. He missed it. Whereas Denver could have been leading 17–7 or 13–7, the Giants took over and grabbed the momentum.

New York scored two points on a safety late in the quarter. With time running out in the half, Karlis missed a second field goal attempt. At halftime, although Elway had completed 13 of 20 passes for nearly 200 yards, Denver led by one point, 10–9.

The Broncos' failure to convert from the one-yard line and to complete the two field goals was a bad omen. In the second half, the Giants took the opening kick and drove the length of the field for a touchdown and a 16–10 lead. Then the Broncos were forced to punt after only three plays as the energized Giants suddenly shut down the Bronco passing attack. New York got the ball back and scored another touchdown. Denver couldn't do anything and punted without making a first down. The Giants quickly scored another touchdown. The rout was on.

New York scored 30 unanswered points and rolled to a 39–20 victory. Phil Simms completed 22 of 26 passes. Elway connected on only 9 of 17 throws in the second half. Late in the game, Coach Reeves pulled him from the game and put in backup Gary Kubiak.

The Broncos players and fans were stunned at the quick turnaround and crushing defeat. In the locker room after the game, Elway's face was blank.

"I felt like I did everything I could," he said. "In the second half they just beat us. There's nothing else to it."

As difficult as it was, Elway and the Broncos spent the rest of the winter trying to put the game behind them. When they returned to training camp in the summer of 1987, their goal was to return to the Super Bowl.

They opened the season with a rush by blasting the favored Seattle Seahawks 40–17 in the first game. John Elway did everything in the game: he passed for more than 300 yards, made several strong runs, and even saved a touchdown by making an open-field tackle after a fumble.

Yet as the season progressed, it became obvious that little had changed from the previous year. Elway was still the key to the Broncos' success, and the team still had trouble running the ball and keeping the opponents from the end zone.

With a disappointing 4–3–1 record in midseason, Elway and Shanahan urged Reeves to make some changes. He grudgingly agreed, and the Broncos adopted the shotgun formation as their basic offensive setup. Since they weren't running the ball effectively anyway, and the opposition already knew that the Broncos had to pass, Elway and Shanahan thought they might as well begin in a passing formation.

The change worked wonders. Denver won six of their last seven games to win the division once more. In the playoffs, they defeated Houston 34–10, then faced Cleveland in a rematch for the AFC championship.

This time the game was played in Denver. The Broncos bolted into the lead, taking a 21–3 lead into the locker room at halftime.

But Cleveland came out on fire in the third quarter and scored an early touchdown. Elway responded with an 80-yard touchdown bomb to receiver Ricky Nattiel, but the Browns came roaring back and scored three more touchdowns while the Broncos managed only a single field goal. It looked like the second half of Super Bowl XXI all over again.

But this time the Broncos, and Elway, came back. In the fourth quarter he threw a touchdown pass to Sammy Winder to put the game away. Denver won, 38–33.

Meanwhile, despite playing erratically for most of the year, the Washington Redskins won the NFC championship. In the playoffs, they barely squeaked by Chicago and, later, Minnesota. The Broncos entered Super Bowl XXII favored by three and a half points.

Denver kicked off but quickly forced the Redskins to punt. The Broncos took possession on their own 53-yard line.

On the first play from scrimmage, Elway took the ball in the shotgun. He looked to one side and waited to see if Redskin cornerback Barry Wilburn would try to anticipate the play. When he did, following Elway's glance to the far side of the field, the quarterback turned and threw to the opposite side, where he hit Ricky Nattiel in midstride. The receiver romped into the end zone to put Denver ahead 7–0 after only one minute and 57 seconds of play.

Washington couldn't move the ball and Denver took over again. This time, the Broncos tried something different.

Elway took the ball and gave it to running back Steve Sewell. As Sewell ran around the end, Elway trotted in the opposite direction, then suddenly turned upfield.

With the defense in hot pursuit, Sewell stopped, planted his feet, and threw a pass to Elway! Elway caught the ball and rumbled for a 23-yard gain. Moments later, Rich Karlis converted a 24-yard field goal, giving Denver a 10-point lead. Even though Elway's pass to Nattiel was his only completion of the day so far, the Broncos seemed to be in command.

But at the beginning of the second quarter, the game completely changed. In a stunning reversal, over a six-minute period Washington quarterback Doug Williams threw for four touchdowns and handed off for another. At halftime, the bewildered Broncos trailed, 35–10.

With such a big lead, the Redskins could afford to play aggressively. In the second half they intercepted Elway three times.

In the huddle, the fiery quarterback was uncharacteristically quiet, appearing just as stunned as his teammates. "He plays better when he's screaming at people," said Mark Johnson after the game. "Usually if you screw up, he'll tell you. And we were really screwing up. For some reason, he didn't go crazy. John was too controlled today."

There was no comeback, and the game went to the Redskins. For the second time in two years Elway had to face the press after failing to come through in the biggest game of his career. Once more, he hardly knew what to say. "We were up 10–0. We had momentum. Then it all caved in," he said, stating the obvious.

"But I also know a lot of quarterbacks never get to the Super Bowl," he added. "In my career, the ultimate is to win this game. That's my ultimate goal. I will not have a good feeling about myself until I win one."

No one, not even Elway, had any idea how long that was going to take.

Chapter Eight:
1988–1989

Another Super Disappointment

Despite his disappointing performance in the Super Bowl, Elway collected a host of individual awards after the season that anointed him the best quarterback in the game. The Associated Press named him the NFL's Most Valuable Player and he was selected as the starting quarterback in the Pro Bowl, where he led the AFC to a win over their NFC rivals. But without a Super Bowl ring, those achievements were hollow. Observers began comparing Elway to Minnesota's Hall of Fame quarterback Fran Tarkenton, an exciting scrambler and terrific passer whose career was never capped by a Super Bowl win, despite four attempts by his Vikings team.

No one was surprised when Elway and the Broncos slumped in 1988. The team's defense, which had probably played over its head during the two Super

Bowl seasons, failed miserably. Former Cowboy running back Tony Dorsett, acquired to bolster Denver's anemic running attack, had no more success in finding holes than his predecessors.

Everything depended on Elway, but this season he couldn't keep the Broncos from falling back. He missed Shanahan, who had left the club after Dan Reeves charged that he and Elway were making changes on offense without his consent. To make matters worse, Elway was beset by a series of nagging injuries all year long. The club lost three of its first four games and never recovered. They finished the season a disappointing 8–8, one game behind the Western Division champion, the Seattle Seahawks.

Although Elway threw for over 3,000 yards and 17 touchdowns, he also threw 19 interceptions. In the fourteen-team AFC, the 1987 MVP was rated the conference's ninth-best passer, eighteenth in the league overall.

On top of everything else, Elway's relationship with Reeves had continued to deteriorate. But after the season, Broncos owner Pat Bowlen gave Reeves a vote of confidence and offered him a new four-year contract. Bolstered by the security of the new deal, Reeves made some changes before the 1989 season. He replaced half of the team's twenty-two starting players, and he fired his defensive coordinator and brought in the highly regarded Wade Phillips to retool the defense.

Spurred on by the play of rookie running back Bobby Humphreys and safety Steve Atwater, the Broncos opened the 1988–1989 season by winning six of their first eight games. Yet Elway was playing the worst football since his rookie season.

Now, no matter what he did, frustrated Broncos fans and Denver's oppressive local media found some reason to complain about Elway. Elway, who owned several car dealerships, was even criticized for his involvement in business. As his performance slipped, his critics complained that his off-field activities proved that he wasn't serious about football and really didn't care about winning or losing. His erratic play early in the season seemed to support such criticism.

Elway's critics didn't understand that most of his problems stemmed from working with a nearly new offensive line. Elway didn't help matters by withdrawing and sniping back at the critics. Despite engineering several comebacks with last-minute heroics, Elway continued to catch flak.

In mid-October, after he was fired as coach of the Los Angeles Raiders, Mike Shanahan accepted Reeves's offer to return and work with Elway. Reeves knew that although the Denver defense had developed into a Super Bowl–quality unit, without Elway the team would have no chance in the playoffs.

Shanahan's return settled Elway down. He began to play more consistently, particularly in a 41–14 Bronco win over Seattle, which raised Denver's record to 10–2. Then out of nowhere, the team slumped.

They lost three of their last four games to finish 11–5, good enough to win the division championship again, but not the way to enter the postseason. Hardly anyone gave them much of a chance to reach the Super Bowl for the third time in four years.

But in the first round, against Pittsburgh, Elway led the team on a second-half comeback. The retooled defense stymied the Steelers, and Denver won, 24–23. The victory set up yet another tussle with the Cleveland Browns for the AFC championship.

The Browns were determined to finally beat the Broncos. John Elway had another idea. He played one of the best games of his career.

In the second quarter, nursing a slim 3–0 lead, Denver had the ball on the 30-yard line. Elway took the snap and went back to pass.

Denver's pass protection broke down and Elway scrambled to his right, buying time. As Cleveland linebacker Clay Matthews bore down, Elway skipped away and threw side-armed off the wrong foot.

The ball sailed downfield like a missile, straight and true, into receiver Michael Young's hands. Young loped into the end zone for a 70-yard score. No other quarterback in the game could have completed the pass. Elway made it look easy.

Later, he scrambled away again and made a 53-yard completion to Vance Johnson. Then he threw a 39-yard touchdown strike to Sammy Winder while on a dead run. Denver won, 37–21, in what Elway later called the "game of my life." He and the Broncos were going back to the Super Bowl.

So were the NFC champions, the San Francisco 49ers. Led by quarterback Joe Montana, the 49ers had already won three Super Bowls during the decade and were generally considered to be one of the greatest teams in NFL history. Montana, despite a weaker throwing arm than Elway, was considered the game's greatest quarterback. With three Super Bowl rings, it was hard to argue with his record.

The powerful 49ers had finished the regular season 14–2. They then blasted Minnesota 41–13 and the Los Angeles Rams 30–3 to win the NFC championship. They were big favorites to win the game.

In the two weeks between the AFC Championship Game and the Super Bowl, John Elway found himself on the defensive. He was hounded by questions about his play in the previous two Super Bowls and by comparisons with Montana. With running back Bobby Humphreys hampered by two broken ribs suffered in the AFC Championship Game, Elway knew that the 49ers were going to come after him. To win, he absolutely had to play a near-perfect game.

When the game began on the afternoon of January 29, 1990, at the Superdome in New Orleans, it was clear that John Elway was feeling the pressure. The first two times he went back to pass, he fired the ball straight into the ground, yards short of his wide-open receivers. The Broncos were forced to punt.

49er quarterback Joe Montana didn't feel the pressure. Or if he did, he didn't let it show. He picked apart the Denver defense with clinical precision.

After the punt, Montana moved the team smartly down the field and threw a 20-yard touchdown strike to Jerry Rice to give San Francisco a 7–0 lead. After the kickoff, Elway seemed to get back on track, only to stall on the 49er 25-yard line after throwing three consecutive incompletions. Denver had to settle for a field goal.

After the two teams each failed to move the ball on their next possession, Montana took control, throwing another touchdown pass just before the end of the first quarter. San Francisco led, 14–3.

Elway couldn't catch them. With Humphreys hurt and the Broncos already far behind, Denver had little choice but to throw on nearly every down. San Francisco's backfield locked down Elway's receivers, while the line went into an all-out rush.

Time and time again, Elway misfired. At halftime,

San Francisco led, 27–3. Elway had completed only six passes.

The rout was on. Elway's first pass of the second half was intercepted, and one play later Joe Montana threw another touchdown pass to Jerry Rice. When Denver got the ball back, another interception of an Elway pass led to another 49er touchdown. Later, Elway fumbled while being sacked and San Francisco returned the dropped ball to the one-yard line.

Although Elway scored the Broncos' only touchdown on a short run, his performance in the eventual 55–10 defeat was humiliating. He completed only 10 of 26 passes for barely 100 yards. His counterpart, meanwhile, was magnificent. Joe Montana was 22 of 29 for 297 yards and five touchdowns.

For the third time in four seasons, Elway tried to explain the inexplicable. He couldn't. None of the Broncos could. They had been outplayed in every facet of the game. "This is going to live with me," said a dejected Elway. "I know that."

Chapter Nine:
1990-1996

Trying to Come Back

The next several years of John Elway's career were marked by occasional spectacular play but eventual disappointment. Nearly every season, he engineered several remarkable comebacks, yet was unable to bring the Broncos back to the Super Bowl.

At the beginning of the 1990 season, Reeves underwent heart surgery, and the team was wracked by injuries, particularly on defense. Elway tried to make up the difference, but after Bobby Humphreys was injured one month into the season, the situation turned hopeless.

Now the opposition began staging comebacks and Denver suffered a series of excruciating, narrow defeats. They tumbled to a 5–11 record.

But the club bounced back in 1991. Coach Reeves, who previously had called the plays, turned that responsibility over to Elway. The strategy seemed to work, for although Elway threw for only 13 touchdowns in 1991, the Broncos finished the regular season with a 12–4 mark to win yet another division title. Elway and Reeves got along better than they had in years.

However, winning the division title was one thing and advancing to the Super Bowl was something else. To advance, they first had to defeat the tough Houston Oilers in the first round of the playoffs. And John Elway was bothered by a sore right shoulder. Once again, the Broncos were underdogs.

The game was close and hard fought. Houston jumped out to an early 10–0 lead, but the Broncos came back to score a touchdown. Unfortunately, they missed the extra point when backup quarterback Gary Kubiak, who had decided he was going to retire at the end of the season, muffed the hold.

Mistakes like missed extra points usually prove costly. Houston made sure that Denver paid the price. As the game entered its final minutes, Houston led 24–23.

Houston punted and Denver took over on their own two-yard line. Slightly more than two minutes remained in the game, and the Broncos didn't have a time-out. The situation looked as hopeless as any John Elway had ever faced.

Yet as he prepared to go onto the field, Gary Kubiak looked at Elway and said, "Pick me up." He was referring to the botched hold earlier in the game. Kubiak had served as backup for most of Elway's career, and also was his best friend on the team. "As I was walking out there," Elway admitted later, "I was thinking we can't let him end his career on a bobbled snap."

On the first play, Elway threw a bee-bee to receiver Michael Young for a 22-yard gain, giving the Broncos some room to operate. But on the next three plays, Denver went nowhere, setting up a fourth-down-and-six situation.

The game, and the season, was down to one play. If Houston got the ball back, Denver would be unable to stop the clock.

Elway took the ball, rolled out, faked a pass, and then decided to improvise. He put the ball under his arm and set his sights on the first-down marker on the sidelines. He dashed around the end, held the ball out, and dove for the marker just as he was swarmed. The official signaled first down!

Playing hard, the Oilers snuffed out the next three plays, setting up yet another fourth down. With 59 seconds left to play, the Broncos were still 65 yards away from the end zone.

Elway took the ball in the shotgun, dodged the rush, and from a dead run tossed a wobbly pass toward receiver Vance Johnson. It wasn't pretty, but it got there.

Johnson was alone. He gathered in the pass and ran upfield, picking up 44 yards before being pushed out of bounds on the 21-yard line.

That was enough. One play later kicker David Treadwell gave Denver the win with a 28-yard field goal.

Afterward, Elway was happy, but he knew the victory was only one game. "I don't know of a better feeling for a quarterback to have," he said. Then he added, thinking about the Super Bowl, "If there is one, I'd like to feel it — in a couple of weeks. I have a vision of getting a perfect team and winning a Super Bowl, and if it means I have to go ten times and get beat ten times, I will. I just want another chance to win it."

But a week later, that vision was put off. In a defensive battle against Buffalo, Elway was forced from the game with a bruised thigh, and Denver lost, 10–7. It was wait-'til-next-year time for Elway.

And next year was a disaster. Elway hurt a tendon in his shoulder and missed several games. The Broncos slumped to 8–8.

The Broncos owners had seen enough. Dan Reeves was fired and replaced by Wade Phillips.

Although the relationship between Elway and Reeves had improved in the past seasons, Elway wasn't disappointed to see him go. He hoped Phillips would finally unleash the offense. Phillips did. For the first time since Elway entered the league as a rookie, in 1983, the team took a different approach.

Phillips hired Jim Fassel as offensive coordinator. Years earlier, Fassel had helped coach Elway at Stanford, and the quarterback was pleased with the selection. Fassel installed the so-called West Coast offense, a pass-oriented attack popularized by the 49ers.

Elway responded by throwing for a career-high 25

touchdowns in 1993, earning him the AFC Most Valuable Player award. Even so, the Broncos narrowly missed making the playoffs. Still, Elway believed the team was improving.

But the injury bug struck again in 1994. The team lost its first four games, seemed to get back on track in the middle of the season, then collapsed to a dismal 7–9 mark. Elway missed two of the final three games with a sore knee.

After the season, Phillips was fired. The Broncos hired Mike Shanahan to replace him.

Elway was ecstatic. In the off-season, Shanahan retooled the West Coast offense, adapting it specifically for Elway. He recognized that although Elway was now a twelve-year veteran, he still had the strongest arm in the league and was the most mobile quarterback in the game. "For a quarterback, it's like dying and going to heaven," said Elway enthusiastically. With the addition of rookie running back Terrell Davis, the Broncos had a more potent offense in 1995 than they had had in years.

Elway led the league with nearly 4,000 passing yards and threw for a career-high 26 touchdowns. Davis, whom Elway called "the best running back

I've ever played with," rushed for over 1,000 yards. Only the Broncos' defense failed to improve, and the team finished 8–8, a record that satisfied no one.

The team began the 1996 season determined to improve. They did, blasting through the regular season with a 13–3 mark as the defense finally started to catch up with the offense. Elway, relaxed and happy under Shanahan, was spectacular all season long. On October 27, in a 34–7 win over Kansas City, he ran and passed for a combined total of almost 350 yards, becoming only the second quarterback in NFL history to accumulate more than 40,000 yards passing and 3,000 yards rushing. But even though Elway's statistics made him a certain Hall of Famer, one achievement still eluded him — a Super Bowl win.

With five weeks remaining in the season, the Broncos clinched a berth in the playoffs. Surprisingly, that was the worst thing to happen to the team all year. Without a goal to shoot for, they lost their edge during the final weeks of the season. With three weeks remaining in the regular season, and Elway sidelined by a minor hamstring pull, Denver was blown out by Green Bay, 41–6. He returned the next week and led the team to their thirteenth win, then played sparingly in the final game, a loss to San Diego.

Despite their loss of momentum, Denver entered the playoffs as odds-on favorites to make it back to the Super Bowl. That seemed even more likely when the Jacksonville Jaguars, in only their second year in the league, upset the Buffalo Bills in the wild-card game. The Jaguars were a good young team, but no one gave them much of a chance against the Broncos, particularly because the game was being played in Denver, where the Broncos were nearly unbeatable.

Denver had had a few weeks off before the playoff game. Although they entered the game well rested, they were also more than a little rusty. Their kicker, Jason Elam, missed a point after touchdown, and Elway's receivers dropped a number of passes.

Meanwhile, Jacksonville quarterback Mark Brunell was playing like Elway usually did — scrambling and making spectacular passes. Brunell kept the Broncos' defense on their heels the entire game. The last six times the Jaguars got the ball, they scored three touchdowns and three field goals.

Despite playing well, Elway and the Broncos just

couldn't keep pace. When the game ended, they were on the wrong end of the 30–27 score. Jacksonville was going to the AFC championship. The Broncos were going home.

After fourteen seasons in the NFL, maybe John Elway just wasn't meant to win a Super Bowl.

Chapter Ten:
1997

That Championship Feeling

In spite of the loss, John Elway had worked too long and hard to give up. But over the past few seasons, his powerful right arm and shoulder had begun to give him trouble. Although few noticed, Elway knew he wasn't throwing the ball with his usual authority.

In the 1997 off-season he underwent minor surgery on the shoulder to clean out loose particles of tissue. But when he began training camp, his arm felt even worse than before. He could barely straighten it.

Then in an early August exhibition game against the Miami Dolphins, Elway made a throw and felt something snap. It didn't hurt, but he left the game holding his right arm gingerly.

Team doctors examined the arm and discovered

that he had ruptured the tendon that connected his bicep — the large muscle on the front of the upper arm — to his shoulder. In fact, they could see where the tendon, after breaking, had sprung back and rolled up like a rubber band near his armpit.

Elway didn't know what to think. If he had surgery again, his season was over. And without surgery, the doctors told him he wouldn't be able to throw.

Then something strange happened. Elway noticed that after the tendon ruptured, his arm didn't hurt anymore. He could straighten it without feeling any pain. When he told the team doctors that his arm felt better than it had in years, they were skeptical. He should have been in pain. When Elway told them he thought he could still throw the football, they were shocked. They could hardly believe he could lift his arm over his head, much less throw a football.

The Broncos put Elway through a secret workout to see if he could throw again. If he couldn't, they didn't want anyone telling the press about it.

Elway slowly warmed up. With each throw he threw the football a little farther and a little harder.

Soon he was throwing his usual bullets 70 yards through the air.

The doctors scratched their heads and pronounced him fit. They didn't quite understand how it was possible, but it was obvious that Elway could still throw the football. They later concluded that the tendon had been deteriorating for so long that the other muscles and tendons in John's arm had compensated for it. He didn't really need the tendon anymore.

Broncos fans breathed a huge sigh of relief when they found out. After the disappointing loss to Jacksonville in the playoffs, they needed some good news.

The Broncos looked sharp during the preseason and continued their fine play in the regular season. Elway played as well as — or better than — he'd ever played. So did running back Terrell Davis, who emerged as the best running back in pro football.

But after surging to a 9–1 start, the Broncos stumbled. On November 16, 1997, in Kansas City, their defense, which had been solid all year, broke down during the game's final minutes. The Chiefs' kicker, Pete Stoyanovic, booted a long field goal to beat

Denver, 24–22. Three weeks later, in Pittsburgh, the Broncos played terrible football in a 35–24 loss to the Steelers. Denver's receivers dropped a total of 11 passes in the contest.

Elway was livid after the game. "We've won a lot of football games, but we've got to learn to win the big one," he said.

One week later, they had another chance in San Francisco during a Monday night game against the 49ers, who were playoff bound again. But when Terrell Davis was forced from the game with a mild shoulder separation, Denver lost their composure. Linebacker Bill Romanowski spit in the face of 49er receiver J. J. Stokes and was later fined $7,500.

The incident spawned a controversy, for some Broncos players believed that Romanowski, who is white, would have been fined a greater amount were he black. The dispute threatened to tear the team apart at the most critical point of the season. Romanowski apologized profusely, and Elway challenged his teammates to put the incident behind them.

In the final week of the season, Denver blasted

San Diego 38–3. But at 12–4, they finished second in the division to Kansas City. They qualified for the playoffs, but only as a wild-card team, which meant they had to play an extra playoff game on the road. That made the task of winning the Super Bowl even more difficult. Only one wild-card team had ever won the Super Bowl.

They faced their nemesis, the Jacksonville Jaguars, in the first playoff game. Terrell Davis, fully recovered from his shoulder injury, was almost unstoppable in the first half. He rushed for two touchdowns to give Denver a 21–0 lead just minutes into the second quarter.

But Jacksonville didn't give up. Mark Brunell rallied his team, and at the beginning of the fourth quarter, the score was 21–17.

The Jaguars then drove down the field to the Denver 16-yard line. Looking to score, Brunell called an audible. But he dropped the snap from the center.

Bronco linebacker Allen Aldridge pounced on the ball and Denver took over. On their second play, Davis rumbled for a 59-yard run and the Broncos scored 21 unanswered points to put the game away. They were one step closer to their goal.

Now Denver faced the Chiefs in Kansas City. The Chiefs were narrow favorites. It was a tough, close contest, the epitome of playoff football. Neither team backed down. Midway through the third quarter, Kansas City led, 10–7.

It was Elway's turn to shine. He drove the team to midfield and then hit receiver Ed McCaffrey on a 43-yard pass that put the ball on the one-yard line. Davis bulled in for the score, and the Broncos' defense made the touchdown stand up. Denver won, 14–10.

The victory earned Denver the right to play the Pittsburgh Steelers in Pittsburgh for the AFC championship.

Both teams started slowly. On the second play of the game, Elway threw an interception. Pittsburgh then drove to within field goal range, but missed. On Denver's second possession of the game, Davis broke loose for a 53-yard gain, Elway then connected on three straight passes, and Davis eventually scored from the eight-yard line to give Denver a lead, 7–0.

But Pittsburgh's young quarterback, Kordell Stewart, was a formidable opponent. He reminded many longtime fans of the young John Elway, for he was both a dangerous passer and a terrific runner. On the next series, he swept the right end on a 33-yard run to tie the score. He then led the team to a second touchdown early in the second quarter to lead by seven points.

Elway couldn't afford to wait until the fourth quarter to mount a comeback. He had to do it now.

A field goal cut the lead to four. Then, with less than five minutes remaining in the half, the Broncos intercepted a pass by Stewart and took over at their own 20-yard line.

Elway was about to prove once again that there was no better quarterback in the game when the clock was ticking.

He hit three straight passes to move the ball to the Pittsburgh thirty-seven. Then, after an incompletion, the Steelers were penalized for interference, giving Denver the ball at the fifteen. Elway calmly drilled a pass to Harold Griffith for a touchdown.

With just under two minutes left in the half, everyone expected the Steelers to run down the clock and regroup. But trailing by only three, 17–14, Steelers coach Bill Cowher wanted to try to score. Stewart failed to connect on three passes and Pittsburgh was forced to punt. Denver took over at their own 46-yard line.

Less than two minutes was plenty of time for John Elway. Another interference call gave Denver 34 yards, then Davis ran for 10 and Elway passed to the one. After Davis was stopped for no gain, the Broncos called their last time-out with only 16 seconds remaining in the half.

After time in, Elway stood behind the center and scanned the Steelers' defense while barking out the signals. Then he took the snap and dropped back.

The Steelers line pressed forward. Elway's receivers cut into the end zone. He spotted Ed McCaffrey and threw a strike.

Touchdown Denver! They stormed into the locker room with a 24–14 lead.

The second half was a defensive struggle. Both defenses played well. Neither broke until the final minutes, when Stewart threw a touchdown pass.

But it was too late. Mixing the occasional pass

with runs by Davis, Denver ran out the clock for the 24–21 win.

John Elway and the Broncos were headed to the Super Bowl for the fourth time. This time, they hoped for a better result.

Chapter Eleven:

1998

Super Satisfaction

Even though the Broncos had reached the Super Bowl by beating three tough opponents on the road, hardly anyone gave them much of a chance against the defending champion, the Green Bay Packers, who had defeated the New England Patriots 35–21 in Super Bowl XXXI. By game time, the Packers were favored by nearly two touchdowns.

Quarterback Brett Favre was the big reason. The reigning NFL MVP was thought by many to be the best player in the game. A brash, swashbuckling, hard-nosed competitor, Favre was blessed with a strong, accurate arm and a unique ability to scramble and make a big play. Packer running back Dorsey Levens was one of the best in the NFL, and veteran defensive end Reggie White anchored an aggressive, physical defense.

In comparison, the Broncos seemed to lack that kind of clout. Although Elway was always a threat and Davis was the game's best runner, Denver's offensive line was physically one of the smallest in the league and given little chance against Green Bay's giants. And the Denver defense was considered little more than average. Besides, the Broncos had a track record of failure in the Super Bowl.

Yet football fans around the country made Elway and the Broncos sentimental favorites. After watching Elway make comeback after comeback over his fifteen-year career, they didn't want to see him fail again. In the days before the game, Elway received hundreds of good luck charms. Even Packer quarterback Brett Favre had to admit that, "If I wasn't playing against him, I'd be pulling for him."

Amidst the hype that generally marks the two-week period between the conference championships and the Super Bowl, Elway was strangely calm. He didn't dwell on his team's past failures. After all, apart from himself, only a handful of his teammates had played on Denver's other Super Bowl squads. They weren't afraid of failure. As the team's elder statesman and leader, Elway knew they looked to him to set the tone. By focusing on the task at hand and exuding confidence, he helped his teammates. None of them felt like underdogs.

At the same time, Elway was well aware of what the game meant for him personally. More than anything else, he wanted to win and secure his place as one of the greatest football players. "In the long run," he admitted before the game, "how you go down in history is measured by how many Super Bowls you win."

Super Bowl XXXII was played at Qualcomm Stadium in San Diego on January 25, 1998. The stands were packed with 68,912 fans, and millions more watched from around the world. But only a few minutes after the opening kickoff, millions of John Elway fans began to get a bad feeling. It looked like Denver was headed for another Super Bowl bust.

Green Bay took the opening kickoff and Favre soon started picking the Broncos apart. Levens was running at will and the Broncos' defense seemed powerless to stop him. The Packers drove 76 yards, including a 22-yard touchdown pass to Antonio Freeman. Green Bay led 7–0 before the Broncos ever touched the ball. Favre and the Packers appeared unstoppable.

But John Elway didn't panic. He knew the best way to beat Green Bay was to keep the Packers' offense off the field.

The Broncos returned the ball to their own 42-yard line. Then Elway started handing the ball to Terrell Davis. He pounded the ball inside over and over again. Denver's offensive line, while small, was quick. They dominated the line of scrimmage.

Even though Elway connected on only one of three passes, the Broncos still managed to drive the ball downfield. Davis punched over from the one and the score was tied.

The Packers took the kick and Favre passed for a short gain on the first play. But his next pass was picked off by Denver at the Packer forty-five. Once more, Elway turned to Davis.

Davis ran for 16 yards on the first play. Then Elway passed for another 9 yards before giving the ball to Davis again. Four plays later, Davis was stopped at the five-yard line and was shaken up when he was accidently kicked in the head. He had to leave the game with a blinding headache. But that didn't stop the Broncos. Two plays later, Davis returned and acted as a decoy as Elway scored on a bootleg.

Then Denver got lucky. Soon after Green Bay got the ball back, Favre fumbled and the Broncos recovered. Normally, Elway would have handed the ball off to Davis again. But Davis was back on the sidelines. Elway turned to the pass instead.

But the Broncos were as ineffective passing as they were successful in running the ball. They settled for a field goal to increase their lead to 10 points, 17–7. They had Green Bay on the run.

Then midway through the second quarter, Favre got the Packers back on track. Mixing the run and pass to perfection, he ate up the clock and drove the Packers 95 yards for a touchdown. At halftime, Denver led by only three points.

After the rest period Davis was determined to try to play again. On the first play from scrimmage in the second half, Elway handed him the ball. Davis got hit, and the ball dropped from his arms. Green Bay recovered, only 26 yards away from a go-ahead touchdown.

The Broncos had to stop them, and they did. The Packers had to settle for a tying field goal. The score was 17–17.

The two teams exchanged possessions, then Denver took over on the Packers' 10-yard line. Once again, it was the Terrell Davis show, as he repeatedly burst up the middle for big yards. Elway hit the occasional pass to keep Green Bay honest. They drove to the Green Bay sixteen, before the Packers' defense stiffened. On third down, Elway dropped back to pass.

Reggie White stormed in from left end, going for the sack, as Elway desperately looked for a receiver. No one was open.

He could have thrown the ball out of bounds, or taken a sack, both of which would have left the Broncos well within field goal range. But a three-point lead wasn't much against the potent Packers. This was the Super Bowl, and John Elway was tired of losing. He wanted to win.

As White rushed him, Elway skipped forward. The big end pawed at the air. Then Elway saw an opening.

He cut by one tackler and set his sights on the first-down marker. Three Packer defenders converged on him.

Most quarterbacks would have either ducked down or slid along the ground to protect themselves. But John Elway is not like most quarterbacks. He threw his thirty-seven-year-old body into a headlong dive for a first down.

As Elway's body stretched out horizontally in the air, all three men hit him. He spun in the air wildly like the blade of a helicopter. Then, as he came down, he held the ball out with his hands and pushed it out for a first down.

The crowd roared with delight. If anyone still questioned whether John Elway had what it took to win a Super Bowl, that play answered the question for good.

"From that point on," said Bronco linebacker John Mobley later, "I knew we had it. This guy's almost forty years old and he's laying his body on the line."

Receiver Sterling Sharpe put it more simply: "He inspired us."

Two plays later, Davis plunged in for a touchdown. Denver now led, 24–17.

When Green Bay fumbled the ensuing kickoff, it seemed as if the Broncos were on their way to another quick score. But just as quickly, they gave the ball back when Elway threw an interception.

Green Bay took advantage and just moments into the fourth quarter tied the score on a Favre touchdown pass.

The clock ticked and the game remained tied. Denver got the ball on the Green Bay forty-nine with 3 minutes and 27 seconds left to play.

As football fans everywhere knew, there was no better place for the football late in the game than in the hands of John Elway.

The Packers stifled Davis on two runs sandwiched around a 15-yard penalty. Then, on second down and nine, Elway found Harold Griffith for 23 yards and a first down and goal on the Packer eight.

The Packers, with only one time-out remaining, couldn't afford to stop the clock. They needed to save the time-out for when — or if — they got the ball back.

On the next play, the Broncos were called for holding, putting the ball on the eighteen. Then Davis got the ball again and swept around the left for 17 yards. The next time he touched the ball, he scored. Denver led, 31–24.

Green Bay got the ball with less than two minutes remaining. The Broncos' defense held, and the Packers gave up the ball on downs with 28 seconds left in the game.

Elway led the Broncos' offense back onto the field as the crowd roared its approval, cheering for the player and the team that, despite their earlier failures, had kept coming back. As Elway bent over the center, he could hardly hear himself call out the signals. He took the snap, touched his knee to the ground as if in prayer, then started celebrating as the final seconds ticked away.

The crowd provided the countdown. "Three! Two! One!" The game was over. The Broncos had won, 31–24. At long last, John Elway was a Super Bowl champion.

Statistically, Elway had a poor game. He had completed only 12 of 29 passes for 123 yards. On any other day, he would have considered that a lousy performance. But on this day, it was stupendous. Terrell Davis won the game's MVP award. And John Elway got the only award he wanted, the Super Bowl championship.

When asked after the game how he felt, Elway could only smile, look around to his fans and team-mates, and sputter, "I guarantee you, it's three times better than anything I could have imagined." For after three Super Bowl losses, the fourth proved to be the charm.

Matt Christopher

Andre Agassi

John Elway

Wayne Gretzky

Ken Griffey Jr.

Mia Hamm

Grant Hill

Randy Johnson

Michael Jordan

Lisa Leslie

Tara Lipinski

Greg Maddux

Hakeem Olajuwon

Emmitt Smith

Mo Vaughn

Tiger Woods

Steve Young

MATT CHRISTOPHER

The #1 Sports Writer for Kids

Read them all!

All available in paperback from Little, Brown and Company